We Draw Breath from the Same Sky

poems by

Mary Anna Kruch

Finishing Line Press
Georgetown, Kentucky

We Draw Breath from the Same Sky

Copyright © 2019 by Mary Anna Kruch
ISBN 978-1-63534-982-5 First Edition
All rights reserved under International and Pan-American Copyright Conventions. No part of this book may be reproduced in any manner whatsoever without written permission from the publisher, except in the case of brief quotations embodied in critical articles and reviews.

ACKNOWLEDGMENTS

Grateful acknowledgement is made to the editors of the following publications in which some of these poems or version of these poems first appeared:

The Remembered Arts Journal, "Early Morning in Amatrice"
River Poets Journal, "Letter Writing"
Edition 3, "Cathedral"
Plum Tree Tavern, "Autumn Pastoral"
After: Stories About Loss and What Comes Next, "What Lingers"
Mused, "Meditations on Trees"
The Mark Literary Journal, "Still Waiting"
Red Wolf Journal, "Stereoscope"
Credo Espoir, "Sinkholes"

Publisher: Leah Maines
Editor: Christen Kincaid
Cover Art and Design: Jennifer Kruch
Author Photo: Emma Kruch

Printed in the USA on acid-free paper.
Order online: www.finishinglinepress.com
also available on amazon.com

Author inquiries and mail orders:
Finishing Line Press
P. O. Box 1626
Georgetown, Kentucky 40324
U. S. A.

Table of Contents

For My Father, Gidio 1

For My Grandfather, Giacinto 4

Letter Writing 6

Stereoscope 8

Elsie's Room 10

Hearts 12

Pasture Rose 13

What Lingers 14

Cathedral 16

Memorial at Monte Cassino 17

Early Morning in Amatrice 19

Meditations on Trees: Toward Winter Solstice 21

Sunset Gathering 22

Deep-set Footprints 23

Autumn Pastoral 25

Double Mirror 26

Spaces 27

Still Waiting 29

To my parents, Gidio and Betty Jo Scenga, who set the standard for romance—and to my husband, Bob, who carries on the tradition

For My Father, Gidio

I stand at the door
of your childhood home,
and I think to myself,
we draw breath from the same sky.

I seek brown eyes—my eyes—
and arms that draw me in,
offer ageless affection;
I ache for insight
of the abyss that grows
when children leave
and parenti* perish;
I crave broad, Roman faces
twinkling recognition,
voices that croon
dialect,
a sky that enfolds the house
that still holds you and welcomes me.

The door has been removed,
the concrete and stone structure
wide open,
but it is full.
Ancient farm implements rest
where you once did.

Back then, did you look up
into the same night sky,
count the same stars, dream of America—
as I dream of returning to this same spot?

The newer house is concrete,
two floors rather than one, tiled not dirt.

You could have used all these rooms
for your cousins, who had shared the space.
How many of your father's family
have lived in this house, farmed the land,
worked the vineyard and olive grove?
Did you feed and care for the animals?

Vittorio and Pierina build on tradition
as they build onto the house
for a returning son.
They look after the farm,
reduced in size over time—acres sold to survive
droughts and poor harvests, pay bills.
Camilla, Vittorio's mother, has recently died;
all but one child grown, gone,
settled, with families of their own.
The old and new homes stand side by side.
At the inside door to the outdoor kitchen,
plastic strips hang to allow the air to flow,
to welcome the farm dog
and the cat who rides his back.

The stove uses gas not wood;
the store room is stocked with farina,
newly-made pasta, salame,
wine lined up on the shelf,
awaiting sustenance and celebration.
An attached dining room
holds a wooden table
beneath a roof of clay tiles.
Even now there is much to celebrate:
births, holidays, saints' days—
visits from American cousins.

Bread cools on the counter;
fresh basil, sautéed garlic, tomatoes
simmer in the day's sauce.
A simple *insalada mista*** has been prepared.
We sit down for la cena,
finding a table simply set;
red wine, salami, and fresh bread
wait, teasing appetites.

Oh, how I wish you were here.

* *parenti* (Italian: relatives)
** *insalada mista* (Italian: mixed salad)

For My Grandfather, Giacinto

I return to the farm in Pofi
and stand on a slight rise
overlooking acres of olives, grapes, and fields.

Under an open, cloudless sky,
I squint through brilliant sun and imagine you,
old straw hat on your head, hoe in your hand.
The air is balmy with the redolence
of freshly-turned earth.
Your brother, Vincenzo, guides
a horse-drawn harrow a few rows over;
you both started at dawn, feeding the animals,
but you are young and have energy to spare,
even in the afternoon heat.

The same sun that deepened olive brown skin
as Giacinto worked the soil
and pruned the vines a century ago
glows through me now.
I walk along rows of tomatoes, peppers,
admire the grapes and olives—
bless those rays that hold me, body and soul.
Closing my eyes, I hear the sheep,
a tractor hum;
soft wind ruffles olive branches
when work is through.

Returning to the house, you think of dinner,
smell the pasta in red sauce
and crusty bread baked that morning.
You will uncork the wine
that you and Vincenzo made last year,
pour generous glasses for the adults,
small ones for the children.

The work has been hard and the day long,
so you will converse little as you eat.
But as the day cools, you will sit outside with the family,
peel some oranges, handing sections to the children.
Talk with Nonna Luisa will be light,
as the sky moves to navy blue.

Today, as I turn toward the outdoor kitchen,
I know that homemade pasta in red sauce,
warm bread, and wine await me.
After dinner, my cousins, la mia famiglia,
will sit beneath the covered veranda, nibble fruit,
and I will lean into the language of my family,
contributing little—but understanding much.

Letter Writing

Some soldiers thrived on smokes;
my father, Gidio, relied on writing home.
He kept his green, leather-bound
English-Italian dictionary
in his pocket for the best part of his day:
letter writing in Italian
at nightfall.

That small volume, dated 1943,
rests on a shelf in my study;
the letters are gone, but when I hold the dictionary
with its frayed edges and corners turned down,
my heart soars.
I envision how his parents felt
when the posts arrived from the Yukon.
His father Giacinto's heart rose,
as he read to wife Luisa
of Morse Code training
and how Gidio missed Mamma's zupe.

When the posts arrived,
sometimes a week's worth at a time,
Giacinto smiled with pride
at the sight of perfectly-composed, polite Italian—
at home they spoke only in dialect.

And when the posts arrived,
each word in Gidio's careful hand,
his father's heart rose,
as he read about the news
of meeting fair, blue-eyed Betty,
a molto bella WAC
who also served on base in the Yukon.
Gidio was over-the-moon!
Betty was taken with him, too.

Naturally, Luisa wanted Gidio to marry
a girl from the Detroit neighborhood
who could make a good sauce
whom she could bully
and have children baptized—
given saints' names, *per l'amor del cielo!* *

Gidio was far from thoughts of church.

And after the war,
before they were married,
Gidio liked to take his green, leather-bound
English-Italian dictionary from his pocket.
He would search the pages with its corners turned down
and choose the perfect English words
at the best part of day:
letter-writing
his love to Betty
    at nightfall.

* *per l'amor del cielo!* (Italian: for heaven's sake)

Stereoscope

Seventy years ago,
life played out in shades of gray
for my mother,
but she longed to view it in the colors
of the Parks she and my father would see
once they had saved two hundred bucks
for a used roadster.

She had seen Alaska,
but had not yet laid eyes on Denali.
She'd not viewed the multicolored sunrise
over Yellowstone, the outcrops
of Aztec sandstone in Red Rock Canyon,
or Yosemite's Firefall
as the sun hits Horsetail Falls,
illuminating upper reaches
in fiery red.
She would settle for even one of these
as long as Dad was beside her.

So they moved into a small
upstairs apartment above Dad's parents,
did without a car, took the bus,
saved five bucks a month in an envelope marked "Parks."

Although the smell of fried garlic
wafted upstairs, drove her to near insanity—
and although the in-laws spoke "in tongues"
as though she did not exist—
Mom looked past all that.
Soon she'd see the Parks,
far from the old neighborhood;
maybe even move to their own home.

When the first baby arrived in '47,
the road trip was put on hold; but not her dreams.
Dad snapped photos of baby in black and white
then developed them in the hall closet,
hand-coloring them in pencil
to add dimension.

When Baby #2 arrived in spring of '49,
they moved two blocks away
to a house with room for the kids to play.
For her birthday that spring,
Dad bought Mom a View Master.
The accompanying booklet boasted
that one could see "third dimension pictures"
in full-color Kodachrome.
Mom saw Yellowstone,
Red Rock Canyon, Denali, and Yosemite
in vibrant slides of stereoscope,
as she told stories about the national parks
to my brother and sister and to me,
Baby #3.

Elsie's Room

She found her way to the bottom
of a pile of coats
strewn across the bed in the back bedroom,
sometimes called "Elsie's room,"
as Elsie was the youngest to move
away from home.

The overabundance of food,
noisy cousins,
cigarette smoke,
and relatives talking over one another
propelled her to nestle
into the calm of Elsie's room.

Even now, she could envision
downstairs, where Grandma and Mom
washed and dried rose-rimmed plates.
Upstairs, some cousins watched Shirley Temple,
lounging in front of a TV,
whose ample top displayed photos
of both JFK and the Pope;
others pushed baby cousins in strollers
up and down the driveway.

She knew the men would be in the garage,
the strict domain of men,
smoking cigarettes, drinking beer.
They talked Tigers and weighed in on the chance
of a good tomato harvest.
Grandpa's garden near the alley
held the trellis from the family farm,
although the tiny Detroit garden
paled when compared to the fields of Pofi.

She stroked the velvet of men's hats
and drowsed amidst the scented scarves,
she gazed at Grandma's old treadle sewing machine,
imagining her fingers
on the wood-engraved stems and petals
carved on sides and drawers.
Adrift in daydreams,
she stretched, yawned, then burrowed
further into the mound of family wraps.

Hearts

She seldom wore makeup,
instead colored in her lips,
careful to fill in the top of the heart,
when she joined my father
in an anniversary dinner
or she left for work.
The delicate Kleenex blot
signaled that she was going out.
She rarely wore perfume,
yet her emergence from a bath
brought hints of Wood Hue bath powder.
Back then her hair was golden brown,
waved by deftly-placed bobby pins.
I would watch her comb through her curls,
humming Sinatra as she slipped
into a crisp blouse or a twirly-skirt dress
for Dad, who would grab his wallet and keys
off the dresser, looking at her with a grin.
His tall frame, curly black hair,
and bedroom eyes, she had said,
reminded her of Victor Mature.
Many years later, I saw *Androcles and the Lion*
and had to agree.
Beyond the heart-shaped lips and bedroom eyes,
there were dance steps near the high-fi
and garden roses set in a vase
near her lipstick, hairbrush, and photo
of a post-war, just-married couple
with hearts in their eyes.

Pasture Rose

You had asked to see Traverse
one last time in early October;
I cannot recall why
we didn't venture one more look
at the golden, sun-drenched meadow
before the frost took the last pasture rose.
You left an unfinished canvas,
wild roses on barbed wire,
hanging on when you could not.

We had gone in the spring
when petals ripened pink;
a rose plucked that day lay pressed.
On days before the hospital,
we sipped tea from your best cups
set roses in a vase for your return.
As you were wheeled into surgery,
you winked, soft cheeks flushed,
jumped into certain thorns, unafraid.
We held our breath
as you took your last.
Where are you now?
Floating above orchards?
Hovering near the old windmill?
Today I shuffled through autumn
toward the farm's open pasture,
reached into my backpack
for the book that held dry petals
still formed—and wandered
toward the rose of sunset.

What Lingers

As my mother grew older,
she developed a preference for French perfume.
The fragrance followed her
from the bath to her rocking chair
and nestled into the afghan she threw over her knees.
Before her last surgery,
my mother had set out her will—
noting to whom her emerald ring should go,
the contents of the safety deposit box,
and her wish for a simple memorial.
Still, no one ever tells you
about having to take back the gifts you gave,
photographs you framed, birthday cards you sent,
afghan you crocheted.
When my brothers and I entered the house,
it was as though she never left—
here a Sinatra record out of its sleeve,
there an Agatha Christie book open,
peppermint gum tucked into a drawer;
an oil painting of her father's barn
sat unfinished at an easel.
In her closet, blouses and slacks
were arranged by color.
A leather folder on the shelf above
held Dad's first paycheck stub,
a copy of their marriage license,
Mom's army discharge papers,
and the love letters—

I reimagine her in White Horse, Alaska;
winter is lit by young love's kisses
against the white-puffed air.
Loose, yellow photographs
slide out of onion-thin paper,
reveal love wrapped in coats and scarves—
unmistakable heat.

We sell the house, disperse furniture,
divide checks among siblings.
But no one tells you about
the random dial of numbers—
numbers found by fingers as easily
as in years past.
The ring is hollow, empty, unanswered.
A deep longing grows.

But sometimes the creak of her rocking chair
slips into dreams.
Then mornings find my cat fast asleep,
curled into the afghan,
lightly scented with French perfume.

Cathedral

Stained glass of rosebud and mint
arc the study window,
glow chapel-warm in summer,
rest on the cat and me.
Crystals set between petals
attract mid-morning sunlight,
form prismed rainbows
on gladdened walls.

On colder days,
we watch for signs of snow
or glimpse mourning doves
sailing past the icy arc,
listen to strains
of public radio broadcasts,
and possibly pray.

Memorial at Monte Cassino

Our Fiat ascended the mountain
on the narrow ancient road
that lead to Monte Cassino.
The abbey rose ethereal, golden—
un castello in a sapphire sky.

I remember the doves—
how they pecked gently at the ground
and not at each other.
Stark white against emerald lawns,
they hopped on tiny feet
round *i giardini centrali,**
marching with reverence
for ghosts of men and monks.

Tourists held their peace,
took in well-placed boulders rescued from the ruins,
climbed blackened steps,
saw sacred scrolls and the relics of saints
stored in urns beneath cathedral altars—
remnants of the air raid
on blunt display.

We spoke in soft whispers,
took the scale grandi
to basement newsreels—
and with my cousin Vittorio
watched in shock, I in shame,
as American planes obliterated the abbey,
some forty miles from his home.

A cemetery on a hill near the abbey
holds bones of 1500 Polish soldiers
who stormed the bombed-out
Benedictine edifice
in search of Nazis—
but perished under 1400 tons
of Allied bombs.
Graves marked with crosses
and Stars of David rest side-by-side,
spread out, a blanket.

A flock of doves appear
as we look skyward
on our way back up the hill
to the abbey.
From the summit,
we see what the doves saw:
an enormous, emerald cross
surrounding a chapel,
standing guard
above the blanket of graves.

i giardini centrali (Italian: the central gardens)

Early Morning in Amatrice

They who lived on the margins of mountains
showed up in droves to help,
knowing all too well the dangers
of life in towns whose walls dated back centuries.
Calls to family assured us they were unharmed,
yet all felt the aftershocks and imagined the pain
of neighbors to the north.

So they gathered in village squares
in Lazio, Umbria, Marche, and Abruzzo
and in regions left untouched,
bringing blankets, medicine, clothes, and water.
Shopkeepers stored supplies until the roads
through the Apennines could be opened.
In the meantime, volunteers secured helicopters
or caught rides with the Red Cross, just to be there.

Amatrice, a hilltop village in Lazio
and the hardest hit,
was packed with guests at the peak of summer.
It lay in rubble, its main street razed.
Hearts broke again and again
as the death toll rose,
growing heavy with children and the old.
A woman named Maria sat before her destroyed home,
a blanket over her shoulders,
waiting to find what had become of loved ones.
Eventually, she joined the search, held a flashlight.

In nearby Norcia, Benedictine monks were safe,
but because their chapel's foundation crumbled
leaving just an altar, they fled to Rome.
There, the monks stood with Papa Francesco
in St. Peter's Square and felt the earth move,
as they led the pilgrims in unified prayer.
Still the death toll rose.

In Amatrice, as in other villages
along the fault, the bringing of supplies,
the prayers, the search for the missing,
and the wearing of black
will continue for many months.
Still the death toll rose.

Maria rested briefly
then made room on a broken pillar
for a mother wrapped in blood-stained bandages.
A child swaddled in a tablecloth
sat on the ground nearby.
Maria took the child into her arms
and pointed at the sky.
Together, they looked up to see
an acclamation of larks
ascend
out of the dust and bricks.

Meditations on Trees: Toward Winter Solstice

I.
Night's frost caused red maples
to rain their leaves,
stream gold and crimson panes
through marbled sky.

II.
Sunlight warms naked cores,
holds tight to living roots,
steadfast, hardy,
mindful of moon's phases—
internal lights
to candle time's passage.

III.
On its march toward winter,
the sky at dusk
morphs to branched profiles
on a watercolor canvas
before it makes way
for Crescent Moon.

IV.
Light has left the day;
navy blue inks twilight
in elegant black silhouettes
in a skyscape
progressing toward Winter Solstice.

Sunset Gathering

From the side porch of the farmhouse
I spotted smoke down at the pond,
rising from the distant mist
of a familiar sunset gathering.
I viewed the day's fast-fading light
blinking around willows, maples,
abandoned field implements.
Shadows moved around the circle of fire
as cousins and siblings huddled together,
swapping stories,
shaking off end-of-summer chill.
Adults sat on painted-over, rusty chairs;
a few stood, clinging to Stroh's cans,
gleeful in discovery of Joe's secret stash.
Children hoped to push bedtime back
as they crouched near the blaze,
grasping burnt remains
of marshmallows on willow sticks.
Watching from the hill top,
I connected to the laughter
and the barns in deep silhouette
framed by the darkening sky.
I turned toward the house to check on Grandma,
who stayed behind to enjoy quiet.
Inside, a delicate doily spun its way
through thinly-veiled fingers.
Taking up my own crochet bag,
I pulled a chair close to her.
There we sat, often silent,
secure in our own sunset gathering.

Deep-set Footprints

The view from the front door
of our family farm house
reveals a sugar-sparkle snow;
the scene calls me out for a walk.

Wearing chore boots,
I step into other footprints
that have cleared paths, perhaps
on a journey of their own remembrance.
Just north of the house,
buildings erected in the late 1800s
still stand as shelter over the years,
providing cover for birds and barn cats,
long after the years of milk cows.
Today they are my postcard.

Behind the house, no wind or bird call
breaks the air this icy morning.
A few pears cling to branches,
shine like frosty bulbs on a Christmas tree.
Even today's bright sun
cannot convince this fruit to fall.

The old log chicken coop, the original kitchen,
survives some hundred years later;
the stonework and weathered wood
rest like works of 19th century art.
Across the front yard,
the garden lies barren, frozen,
dreaming of spring's attentions.
I stay with the deep-set footprints,
trudging my way to the pond.
To my left, the well house nestles
into the hill for warmth.

At the pond, I wonder at the willows
hanging leafless and low
to the ground, yet still striking,
tapping the pond's ice with their bony branches.

On the walk up the hill from the pond,
I sight the familiar outline
of a handmade hickory bench,
set in the sapphire sky.
Many a summer morning
I have found solitude there, writing,
away from the noise of visiting kin.
On the ground nearby, a simple cross marks
the grave of old Keillor, a beloved farm dog.
The barns and silo hibernate.

In the front yard, old apples remain
on trees, frozen in place,
sticking together like old married folk
through frigid nights and chilly days,
like our late, beloved Dad and Mother.

On the drive back home,
I hold Mom's rosary
that she held many of her last nights.
Tears fall in loss and thanksgiving.

Autumn Pastoral

The pilgrimage begins in early autumn
at the foothills of the Rockies,
where the road shadows the river.
Rock ledges of red and burnt sienna
form terraced altars for juniper and spruce;
harebell and wild flax bloom at their feet.
Past the ledges, the sky is overcast but visible;
Quaking Aspen, linked by one root system,
spread their wings above ground,
find patches between rocks to flourish.
A sharp turn marks a grove of cottonwood
clustered together, leaves fluttering, sharing secrets.
Trail Ridge Road climbs higher into the mist;
we expect saints to appear, point the way.
A sign for Fall River Road comes into view.
Ponderosa Pines fade into thick clouds;
headlights shoot through the fog,
and the road snakes toward Chasm Falls.
Partly-obscured guard rails bend and kneel, lean
toward free-fall disaster, barely three feet to the left.
Poplars gone red emerge, flow, then meld into a baptism
of tangerine alder, juneberry, and spruce.
A dip in the road brings clarity to the clouds,
a veil lifts, log cabins appear,
and plains open up to a herd of elk.
Since we last laid eyes on this spot,
a marriage of years has passed;
we pull over to take in the view:
aspens crown the golden pastoral scene—
and he touches the ring he gave me that day.

Double Mirror

Shawls of subtle rain lie over the trees,
and the community of water fowl
went about their evening swim,
unencumbered by the fall.
I watched from a park bench,
sitting solo after an argument I no longer recall.
The gentle shower had dripped onto my face,
washed it clean of expression
while I observed, damp but profoundly affected—
As the rain ceased,
I saw a sleek pair of adult swans
moving away from shore,
double-mirrored in the silent pool.
The pair embodied a reverse side of their beings,
like humans imparting one image to the world,
keeping another for private study.

Minutes later,
brightly-lit puddles along the banks
glinted like eyes reflecting new sun.
Park visitors who had sheltered
in cars or under storefront canopies
during the light downfall
ambled back to benches and books,
tramping as slowly as sunshine
on reluctant dandelions.
I looked up to find him
returning, almost running;
he said my eyes smiled diamonds.

Spaces

Our days appear full—
he is outdoors,
coaxing life into dry, potted plants
and wilted landscaped roses;
I am indoors,
coaxing words I know by heart
from arthritic fingers—
my mother's hands
   my own
into verse—if not eloquent,
then at least efficient.

I tap keyboard phrases,
grasping bare-bone fragments
of parents so beloved
with moods so unalike
their ghosts consume my thoughts:

   intensified in space.

Our days appear full,
He, out on errands
I, fixed inward,
perusing old post cards
from Italian family,
rereading baptismal records
and legal pad notes in Dad's hand.
I seek answers in deep brown eyes
   my eyes
that stare back from yellowed photos,
set among vineyards.
The space inside
ponders triggers
that stole my father's calm control

when untidy demands
at work and home
raised his voice in anger—
his fist in despair—
shattered glasses,
unleashed demons.

The space inside
craves platters of pasta
and glasses that clink *Salute*
around a table brimmed in cheer,
    and at times tears,
a space resonating
with rich dialect
denied in a half-sane,
    half-American
        childhood home.

He returns, fills a vase
with landscape roses,
pours red for both of us,
clinks *Salute*,
leads me outside into the light.

Still Waiting

I.
When I walked to our meeting place
to wait for you by the river,
it was another 70s evening
for girls with flowers in their hair
and boys lucky enough to snag deferments
or low lottery numbers.

Students strolled by in a restless shuffle
back to dorms for dinner.
Light grew dim, and I waited.

Night classes stirred sandals
into a growing hustle
past the peace sign on the big rock,
past the tents in People's Park.
Still, I waited.

Guitars strummed; leaflets and weed were offered.
A boisterous group with signs
marched to Beaumont Tower.
They had no problem speaking their minds.
But you did.

II.
I thought back to a night
soon after we met.
We sat up until 4 a. m.
under a faint, blue light on your bed
where you spilled what guts you did not lose
on the front lines.
You spoke of women and children—
huts you would not set ablaze,
the surprise attack,
and the men in your company
who were gone—while you lived on.

The war took so much more than your body—
for a time, it took your voice.
As I dared to reveal myself,
you held me at a distance,
masking your face,
closing me out of all
but the most required talk.

Did I misjudge you?
Expect too much?
Push too hard?
I was aware of my naivety;
you who had breathed death.

III.
Still, in the beginning
you had agreed
to walk and talk and just be together.
So I resolved to be patient,
to hold my peace
to give you room
to move beyond my need
to know your mind.

So I waited at our meeting place.
You did not see me
waiting for you by the river.
An hour went by—
and then another.

When at last your headlights
came into view,
you drove right past
without a look in my direction.
Why couldn't you see me
waiting for you by the river?

Branches whispered, entwined
over slow, black water.
The breeze kicked up,
grew cold.

IV.

We are better now.
I learned to leave you alone
in your dark moods,
and we don't always talk with words.

At the river, we did not know
the depth of Agent Orange's
destruction:
leukemia.
Now, infusions restore some lost power;
you stand tall in the growth of our landscape.
Dark times are rare.

Nonetheless, years later
I pass that place and remember
the fear   the hurt   the dread
as crowds of students still head to class,
still gather at Beaumont Tower,
still form a never-ending flow.

I wanted to talk, but you didn't.
See me.
I am still here,
will always be here,
waiting for you.

Mary Anna Kruch is a career educator and full-time writer, inspired by family, nature, and place, particularly her Italian family near Rome, Italy. "To My Father, Gidio," the first poem in *We Draw Breath from the Same Sky,* was written following recent visits to her father's family farm in Pofi, now run by fourth cousin Vittorio, who deeply resembles her father in both looks and temperament. Several poems in the collection reflect life in an Italian-American family and her parents' tender relationship. Two poems are set on her husband's family farm in northern Michigan, and four reflect her 45-year marriage to husband, Bob. The family farms and the beauty of her own backyard provoke both poetry and photography.

Mary Anna has two grown daughters and has written a textbook, *Tend Your Garden: Nurturing Motivation in Young Adolescent Writers*, along with several professional papers. Her poetry has appeared in *The Remembered Arts Journal, River Poet's Journal, The Mark Literary Review, Trinity Review, Credo Espoir, Portage Magazine,* and *Wayne Literary Review*. This is her first poetry collection.

www.ingramcontent.com/pod-product-compliance
Lightning Source LLC
LaVergne TN
LVHW041505070426
835507LV00012B/1332